# 101 Little Known...
# MICHAEL JORDAN

Sports Publishing Inc.
a division of Sagamore Publishing
Champaign, IL

© 1997 Dreaming Dog Publishing
All rights reserved.

Book design: Michelle R. Dressen
Cover design: Julie L. Denzer
Cover photo: Brian Spurlock
Photos: Brian Spurlock, Michael C. Hebert, and Allen Kee

ISBN: 1-57167-149-8

Printed in the United States

www.sagamorepub.com

**1.**
Michael Jeffrey Jordan was born in Brooklyn, New York, February 17, 1963, while his father was attending a training program there for General Electric.

**2.** Michael shares the same birthday as football great Jim Brown (1936).

**3.**
Michael's father, James, worked his way up from forklift operator to a supervisor at General Electric. Michael's mother, Deloris, worked as a clerical supervisor at United Carolina Bank.

**4.**
**Michael is the second youngest of five children—James Ronald, Delois, Larry, Michael and Roslyn.**

**5. According to MJ, who had the greatest influence in his life? "My mother and father."**

## 6.

**The Jordan family moved from Wallace, North Carolina to Wilmington, North Carolina when Michael was five years old. He lived in a two-story tan and brick house on Gordon Road.**

**7.
A seven-mile strip of Interstate 40, north of Wilmington, is named in Michael's honor**

**8.**
MJ had perfect attendance as a first grader at Ogden Elementary School and won an award for best sense of humor at Virgo Middle School.

**9.**
**Michael's favorite childhood memory is being at his grandmother's house on holidays and special occasions.**

**10.**
**MJ's first bicycle was a red Schwinn he got for his 12th birthday.**

**11.**
**As a 12-year-old, Michael threw a one-hitter to win the league title for his Dixie League baseball team. Michael's Babe Ruth team won the state championship with MJ winning MVP honors.**

**12.**
**Why is Michael 6-feet-6? Because his mother used to tell him, "When you go to bed tonight, Mama will pray over you and put salt in your shoes to help you grow."**

**13.**
**Michael was cut in tryouts for Emsley A. Laney High School's varsity basketball team as a sophomore.**

**14.**
MJ wore uniform No. 45 as a junior-varsity player in high school, the same number as his brother Larry was wearing with the varsity. The next year, Larry still had No. 45, so Michael took No. 23 because it is roughly half of 45.

**15.**
Michael intercepted three passes in a high school football game, competed in the high jump and long jump in track and pitched 42 consecutive scoreless innings for the baseball team.

**16.**
MJ was a B-plus student in high school; his favorite subject was math.

**17.**
Michael had to wait tables in exchange for a spot in the prestigious Five Star high school basketball camp in Pennsylvania.

# 18.
Michael sent letters to the basketball staffs at UCLA and Virginia, but the inquiries were never answered.

**19.**
MJ's favorite college team growing up was North Carolina State. He disliked North Carolina, but committed to attend UNC in November 1980.

20.
Michael scored 12 points against Kansas in his first game at North Carolina, November 28, 1981.

**21.**
MJ hit a 17-foot fade-away jump shot with 16 seconds remaining in the game to lead North Carolina to the 1982 NCAA championship as a freshman. Jordan claims he did not see the shot go in.

**22.**
Michael was the leading scorer with 17.3 points per game on the 1983 U.S. Pan American Games team that won the gold medal in Caracus, Venezuela.

**23.**
**Michael was the leading scorer (17.1 points per game) on the 1984 U.S. Olympic team that won the gold medal in Los Angeles; he won a second Olympic gold medal as a member of the U.S. Dream Team in Barcelona in 1992, averaging 14.9 points per game.**

**24.**
Jordan majored in cultural geography at the University of North Carolina. Despite joining the NBA after just three years of college, Michael returned to school in the off-season and earned his Bachelor of Arts degree in December 1986.

**25.
He was the third player chosen in the 1984 NBA Draft, behind Hakeem Olajuwon (by Houston) and Sam Bowie (by Portland).**

**26.**
Said Chicago General Manager Rod Thorn the day the Bulls drafted Michael: "Jordan isn't going to turn this franchise around."

**27.
Michael's first NBA contract was for a total of $6 million paid out over seven years.**

**28.**
Michael scored 16 points against the Washington Bullets in his first game for the Chicago Bulls, October 26, 1984.

**29.**
Michael played his rookie year at 199 pounds; he played at 216 pounds in 1996-97.

**30.**
Michael's 1984-85 rookie-season basketball card, No. 101 in the Star series, is valued at $2,200-$2,900.

**31.**
Nike's Air Jordans were introduced in 1985. The Bulls originally said he couldn't wear them since they didn't match the team's colors. They grossed $110 million in the first year.

**32.**
**Michael wears size 13 shoes. He uses a new pair of sneakers every game and laces every pair himself.**

**33.**
**Michael broke his left foot October 29, 1985 and missed 64 games. He's missed only seven other games in his NBA career.**

**34.** Jordan set an NBA playoff record with 63 points in a 1986 game against the Boston Celtics.

**35.
Michael won two straight Slam Dunk contests at the NBA All-Star Weekend (1987 and '88).**

**36.
Michael scored an NBA-record 23 consecutive points against Atlanta, April 16, 1987.**

**37.**
Jordan and Wilt Chamberlain are the only NBA players to score more than 3,000 points in a season. Jordan had 3,041 points in 1986-87; Chamberlain surpassed 3,000 points three times: 1960-61, '61-62, '62-63.

**38.**
Michael became the only player in NBA history to record 200 steals and 100 blocked shots in the same season. He did it in 1986-87 and again in 1987-88.

**39.**
Michael's statistics as an outfielder for the Birmingham Barons in 1994 were: 127 games, .202 batting average, three home runs, 51 runs batted in, 30 stolen bases, 114 strike outs and 11 errors. He wore uniform No. 45. The specifications of Michael's bats, made by Hillerich & Bradsby: 35 inches long, $33\frac{1}{2}$ ounces, black, model #M216.

**40.**
Michael scored his regular-season career-high 69 points at Cleveland on March 28, 1990. He played 50 minutes, hit 23-of-37 FGs, 2-of-6 3-pt. FGs, 21-of-23 FTs, had 18 rebounds, six assists, four steals, two turnovers and five fouls. The Bulls beat the Cavaliers, 117-113, in one overtime.

**41.
Michael averaged an NBA-record 41.0 points per game in the 1993 NBA Finals series against Phoenix.**

**42.**
**MJ announced his retirement from professional basketball on October 6, 1993. He returned to the NBA on March 19, 1995.**

**43.
Michael was named the NBA's top defensive player in the 1987-88 season.**

**44. Michael's nickname with his Barons teammates was "Kilroy."**

**45.**
In the two weeks prior to his return to the NBA the stocks for companies he endorsed (General Mills, General Motors, McDonald's, Nike, Quaker Oats and Sara Lee) increased in value a combined $3,841,968,170.

**46.**
**Michael's favorite teammate ever was Charles Barkley, when both of them were members of the Dream Team.**

**47.**
Michael's No. 23 Chicago Bulls uniform was officially retired November 1, 1994. It was the third Bulls number retired. The other players so honored are Bob Love (No. 10) and Jerry Sloan (No. 4).

## 48.

Michael has worn uniform No. 23 for most of his career, but he wore No. 45 during his "comeback" season and No. 12 for one game in 1990 when his jersey was stolen out of the team's equipment bag.

**49.
Michael earned $850 in salary a month and $16 in meal money a day for playing minor league baseball.**

**50.**
When Michael returned to the NBA in 1995, his first game back received a national rating of 10.9 on NBC-TV, the highest rating for any regular season game in league history.

## 51.
Michael is one of only two players to win MVP awards in the All-Star Game, regular season and NBA Finals in the same season. He did it in 1996. The other player was Willis Reed of the New York Knicks in 1970.

**52.**
Jordan was paid $30 million for playing the 1996-97 season. That came to $12,340.60 for each of the 2,431 points he scored.

**53.
Michael received a record 2,451,136 votes—out of 8,879,330 ballots cast—for the 1997 NBA All-Star Game.**

**54.**
Michael recorded the only triple-double in NBA All-Star Game history in 1997. He had 14 points, 11 rebounds and 11 assists, but lost the MVP award to Charlotte's Glen Rice.

**55.**
Michael holds the NBA career records for highest scoring average for the regular season (31.7 points per game), playoffs (33.6) and All-Star Game (21.1).

**56.**
**Michael has played for four coaches in Chicago: Kevin Loughery (1984-85), Stan Albeck (1985-86), Doug Collins (1986-89) and Phil Jackson (1989-97).**

**57.**
**In MJ's 12 seasons on the Bulls' roster, Chicago has compiled a record of 599-320 (.652). In the 20 seasons without him, Chicago is 786-836 (.485).**

**58.**
Michael was the league's season leader in steals three times. He ranks third on the NBA's career steals list with 2,165. He trails John Stockton (2,531) and Maurice Cheeks (2,310).

**59.**
MJ has recorded 28 career triple-doubles in regular season games, plus two more in the playoffs. Since 1979, that's the fourth-highest total behind Magic Johnson (138), Larry Bird (59) and Fat Lever (42).

**60.**
**Michael is one of only seven players to win an NCAA championship, NBA title and an Olympic gold medal.**

**61.**
**Jordan has scored 40 or more points 153 times. He's done it against every NBA team except the Toronto Raptors and Vancouver Grizzlies.**

**62.**
MJ has scored 50 or more points 30 times. Only Wilt Chamberlain hit that plateau more often, 118 times.

**63.
Michael has scored in double figures in each of his last 758 games. That streak is second only to Kareem Abdul-Jabbar's 787 games.**

**64.**
MJ is fifth on the all-time NBA career scoring list with 26,920 points. He trails Kareem Abdul-Jabbar (38,387), Wilt Chamberlain (31,419), Moses Malone (27,409) and Elvin Hayes (27,313).

**65.**
Jordan earned $38 million in endorsement deals in 1996 according to the *Sports Marketing Letter.*

**66.**
Bijan manufactures Michael Jordan Cologne. It's made of 18 essences, including cedarleaf, suede and juniper berry. It grossed $75 million in the first six months.

**67.**
The movie "Space Jam," starring Michael and Bugs Bunny, grossed $29.2 million in its first weekend of release.

**68.**
Adults could participate in a three-day Michael Jordan fantasy basketball camp in Las Vegas in the summer of 1997 for $15,000.

**69. Michael has appeared on the cover of *Sports Illustrated* a record 40 times.**

**70.**
*The Jordan Rules,* **by Sam Smith of** *The Chicago Tribune,* **sold 175,000 copies in hard cover and 400,000 in paperback, making it one of the best-selling sports books of all time.**

**71.
Michael's mother, Deloris, wrote a book on child rearing, *Family First: Winning the Parenting Game*.**

**72.**
**The Michael Jordan Foundation awarded grants worth more than $5 million from 1989-96.**

**73.
MJ donated
$1 million to
the University
of North
Carolina's
School of
Social Work.**

**74.**
**The James Jordan Boys and Girls Club and Family Life Center services 1,000 people daily in Chicago.**

**75.**
**Michael married Juanita Vanoy in a Las Vegas wedding chapel during Labor Day weekend, 1989. Juanita was a loan officer at a Chicago bank. She and MJ met at a post-game party at Bennigan's on North Michigan Avenue during his rookie season.**

**76.**
**Michael's favorite arena to play in outside of Chicago is New York's Madison Square Garden.**

**77.**
**The signature dish at Michael Jordan's Restaurant is "Juanita's Mac & Cheese." The ingredients are elbow macaroni, cream, sharp cheddar cheese, Romano cheese, butter, salt and pepper.**

**78.** Michael's greatest joy in life? "Watching my three children: Jeffrey, Marcus and Jasmine."

**79.**
Michael has three dogs, an Akita named Jazebel and two Maltese puppies, Missy and Jasper.

**80.**
Michael got his first set of golf clubs from PGA star Davis Love III when they were students at North Carolina.

**81.
MJ has a putting green in the basement of his home.**

**82.**
**Michael was host of the 1988 television series, "Greatest Sports Legends" and the guest host of "Saturday Night Live," September 28, 1991.**

**83.**
Jordan's primary residence is in Highland Park, a suburb of Chicago, but he also maintains a home on Hilton Head Island.

**84.** Michael's dream golf foursome: "Can I say five? Tiger Woods, Arnold Palmer, Davis Love III, Ben Hogan and me."

**85. Michael gets manicures every 10 days and pedicures once a month.**

86. Michael's favorite musical performers are Anita Baker and Whitney Houston.

**87.**
**Despite being one of the world's greatest athletes, Michael doesn't know how to swim or ice skate.**

**88.**
**Michael wears a pair of North Carolina shorts under his Bulls shorts.**

**89.
MJ has an Omega horseshoe sign branded on his chest for good luck.**

**90.**
Michael averaged 79.8 strokes per round in five Celebrity Golf Association tournaments in 1993, but had a career-best 71 in one tourney.

**91.
MJ said if Colin Powell ever runs for president of the U.S., he would be willing to work for the ex-general.**

**92.
Michael says if he weren't playing pro ball, he'd be a meteorologist.**

**93.
Michael's first part-time job was as a maintenance worker at a hotel.**

**94.**
**MJ says Jerry West is the one player in NBA history he'd like to go against one-on-one.**

**95.**
**MJ received the gift of a silver-dipped sneaker from the owner of Henry Kay Jewelers for his 32nd birthday.**

**96.**
**The husband and wife team of Omri Amrany and Julie Rotblat-Amrany sculpted the 12-foot high statue of Michael in front of the United Center.**

**97.**
Michael prefers to drive a black Ferrari Testarossa with North Carolina license plates that read "MJ AIR 23." Appropriately, the state slogan on the plate is "First in Flight."

**98.**
**The two magazines MJ always reads are** *GQ* **and** *Cigar Aficionado.*

**99.
In 1993, MJ received the best-mannered award from the National League of Junior Cotillions.**

**100.**
**The Michael Jordan Golf Co. owns a golf practice center in Aurora, Illinois, and a retail store in Chicago.**

**101.
Michael owns 150 suits and once spent $200,000 on clothes in a single shopping spree.**

# Also available in the *101 Little Known Facts* series:

# Available at your local bookstore or by calling (800) 327-5557

# Also available in the
# *101 Little Known Facts* **series:**

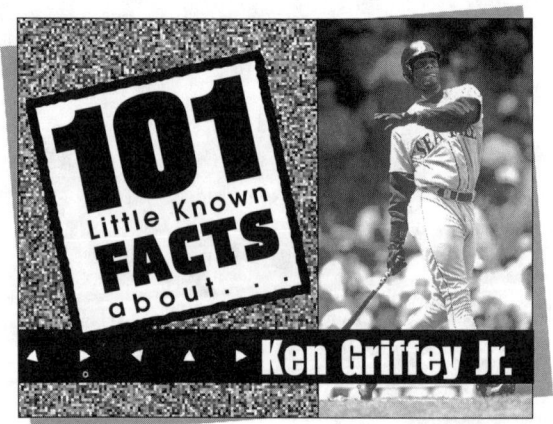

# Available at your local bookstore or by calling (800) 327-5557

# Also available in the
*101 Little Known Facts* **series:**

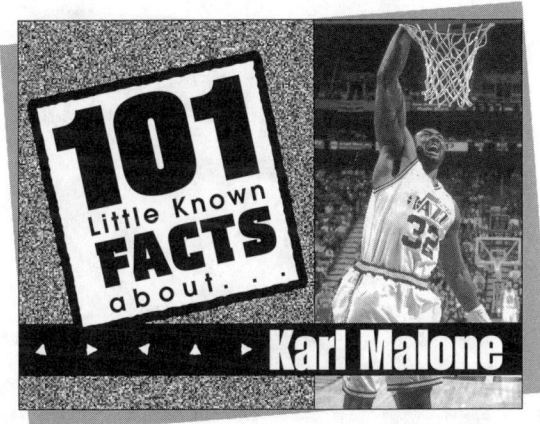

# Available at your local bookstore or by calling (800) 327-5557

# Also available in the *101 Little Known Facts* series:

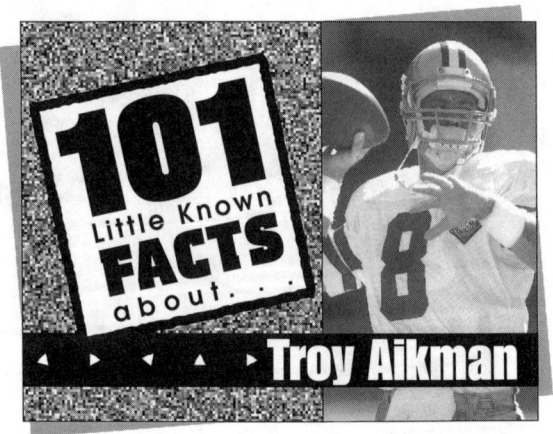

# Available at your local bookstore or by calling (800) 327-5557

**More titles coming soon in the
*101 Little Known Facts* series!**

**For more information, contact
your local bookstore
or call (800) 327-5557**